# LIVE HAPPY

*How to flourish through life with Jesus at the center*

by Marjie Schaefer

www.FlourishThroughTheWord.com

© 2014 by Marjie Schaefer. All rights reserved. No part of this document may be reproduced or transmitted in any form by any means, electronic, mechanical, photocopying, recording, or otherwise, without prior written permission of Marjie Schaefer.

*This Bible study is affectionately dedicated to
the women of the Flourish community.*

*My prayer is that we will all continue to hunger and thirst
for more of Jesus in our lives and more of His Living Word.*

*Knowing Christ in us, the hope of glory,
is our foundational reason for living happy.*

## A note from Marjie before you begin….

Welcome to the wonderful journey through Colossians! This is a power-packed, short 4-chapter book that is destined to change your life, if you let it.

I encourage you to do all of the homework throughout the 7 weeks of this study. Look up each Scripture verse and take the time to thoughtfully answer each question. Each week has 5 days of homework assigned.

Inside you will find Greek words and definitions, along with excerpts from other books that echo the themes of what it means to *Live Happy*. I included these excerpts so that you could see how the principles and truths of God's Word are integrated into all of life. Even a book that isn't necessarily Christian can reflect the transforming truths of life-giving Scripture. Please take the time to read each excerpt as it will enhance your study experience.

Also included are some personal stories and teachings from others that will expand your understanding and experience.

Make the most of these few weeks we will spend together and be sure to prioritize your study time so that you can embrace the Biblical meaning behind *living happy!*

May you drink deeply from the 'well of your salvation' and may Jesus Himself become more real to you as a result of your trip through Colossians!


Living happy with you,

*Marjie*

# LIVEHAPPY
– WEEK ONE –

# HAPPINESS
is not a destination. **It's a way of life.**

# A trip through Colossians
## Day One

The Apostle Paul had never visited the city of Colosse when he wrote this letter. Colosse was about 100 miles east of Ephesus, and the church there was an outgrowth of Paul's three-year ministry in Ephesus.

Epaphras was most likely the founder and pastor of the church in Colossae. The church met in the home of Philemon. Scholars believe Paul wrote this letter during his first Roman imprisonment, around A.D. 61.

With this background in mind, take the time to read the entire first chapter of Colossians today.

Answer the following questions based on your findings:

1. In verses 1-2, what do you learn about Paul, and what does he desire for the church in Colosse?

2. What was Paul's first order of business in this letter, according to verse 3?

3. What did the Colossians have a reputation for based on verse 4?

4. Verse 5 gives the reason for their hope. What 3 things do you see in this verse that affirmed their hope? How are these 3 things the same yet different?

5. The Gospel comes to individuals and the world (v. 6), and when it comes, it brings forth _____.

6. What 'fruit' has come to your life because of the Gospel? *Write out your brief testimony of that fruit here:*

7. Who has been a 'dear fellow servant' and a 'faithful minister' like Epaphras in your life (v. 7)? How have they shown you Christ?

**Day Two**
**Read Colossians 1: 3-8**.

1. Verse 8 is the single reference in this letter to the Holy Spirit.

   Paul wrote to the church in Colossae that Epaphras had declared to him (and his companions) their *'love in the Spirit'*.

   Read Romans 7:6 and write out the verse here:


What 3 things emerge out of Romans 7:6 that reveal aspects of living in the Spirit:

1)

2)

3)


**The Greek word & definition:**

**Spirit,** *Pneuma:* Strong's #4151: that part of a person capable of responding to God. The Holy Spirit... draws us to Christ, convicts us of sin, enables us to accept Christ as our personal Savior, assures us of salvation, enables us to live the victorious life, understand the Bible, pray according to God's will, and share Christ with others.

This definition also includes breath, breeze, a current of air, wind, spirit.

(Hayford, Jack W. *New Spirit Filled Life Bible.* Nashville, TN: Thomas Nelson Bibles, 2002. 1559. Print.)

1. Read also Romans 15:30 and write out another aspect of 'loving in the Spirit' based on this verse.

2. Using the 2 verses in Romans and the Greek definition of Spirit, or *pneuma*, along with Colossians 1:8, write out a brief paragraph describing how you have been loved 'in the Spirit' by other believers. Spend some time giving thanks to God for this gift.

3. Now write a brief paragraph expressing how you seek to love other believers 'in the Spirit' and what that looks like in your life.

## Book Note:

In his book, The Happiness Advantage, professor and author, Shawn Achor reports the results of one of the longest-running psychological studies of all time—the Harvard Men study. This study followed 268 men from their entrance into Harvard in the late 1930's all the way through their late adulthood (40 years). The psychologist who directed the study summed up the findings in one word: **love**.

The years of evidence and data proved that our relationships with other people matter, and they matter more than anything else in the world. The more social support we have, the happier we are. A lifetime of strong social relationships provides crucial protection against the dangerous effects of stress.

<small>(Achor, Shawn. *The Happiness Advantage: The Seven Principles of Positive Psychology That Fuel Success and Performance at Work*. New York: Crown Business. 2010. 175-177. 188. Print.)</small>

4. The Apostle Paul did not need a decades-long psychological study to share the benefits of 'love in the Spirit' with the believers in Colosse! Loving and supportive relationships with others truly is a source of happiness and great joy in our lives.

   Summarize what you have learned from this brief study about loving others in the Spirit and put those findings down in the form of a prayer:

**Day Three**
*A Way to Pray....*
Read Colossians 1:9-12 several times. If you have various translations available to you, read this passage in a few different versions.

1. In verse 9, Paul says they had not ceased to pray for the believers 'since the day they heard it'. Using verse 8 to answer, what was Paul referring to here?

2. Using the specifics listed in verses 9-11, write out the targeted ways Paul prayed for the believers:
    - V. 9:
    - V. 10:
    - V. 10:
    - V. 10:
    - V. 10:
    - V. 11:

3. Spend the rest of your study time today creating a prayer list of those you would like to commit to pray this way in the coming days and weeks.

**Day Four**
*Taking the prayer apart, bit by bit....*

1. Write out Colossians 1:9 here:

2. The phrase *'that you may be filled with the knowledge of His will in all wisdom and spiritual understanding'* is a powerful way to pray for anyone. Look up the following verses and write out the parts from these verses that echo the specific way Paul encouraged us to pray for others:
    - Ephesians 1:15-17:

    - 1 Corinthians 1:5:

    - Romans 12:2:

    - Ephesians 1:8:

3. Using these verses, expand on your understanding of Paul's phrase in verse 9:

4. Write out Colossians 1:10 here:

5. The phrase *'that you may walk worthy of the Lord'* is filled with implications for believers. Look up the following verses and write out the parallel statements:
   - Ephesians 4:1:

   - 1 Thessalonians 2:12:

6. Verse 10 continues with this phrase, *'fully pleasing Him...'*. Look up 1 Corinthians 15:58 for a different perspective on this phrase and write out how the two verses relate to each other.

**Day Five**
**Read Colossians 1:9-12.**

1. Write out verse 10 in its entirety again here:



2. The phrase *'being fruitful in every good work'* is a wonderful way to pray for others. Look up the following verses and write out the coordinating phrases:

    - Hebrews 13:21:


    - Philippians 1:6:


3. Paul wraps up verse 10 with the phrase *'increasing in the knowledge of God'*. Here are some verses that can expand what that means; please write out:

    - 2Peter 1:2:


    - 2Peter 3:18:


4. Write out Colossians 1:11-12 for the final phrase of Paul's prayer:

5. The Greek word and definition:

   **Strengthened,** *Dunamoo:* Strong's #1412: To make strong, confirm, enable.

   (Hayford, Jack W. *New Spirit Filled Life Bible.* Nashville, TN: Thomas Nelson Bibles, 2002. 1671. Print.)

   Using Ephesians 3:16 and Ephesians 6:10, along with the Greek definition, write out your thoughts on how God strengthens believers as we pray this way:

6. Review the last 3 days of your study of Paul's prayer for the Colossians and summarize the Biblical lessons you gleaned from this extensive look at these principles throughout Scripture:

# LIVEHAPPY
### – WEEK TWO –

If you really

want to

## BE HAPPY

no one

can stop you!

# Digging Deeper
**Day One**

Last week, we spent concentrated time on Paul's specific prayer for the Colossians. This week, we will delve in to the theology (the study of God) behind those prayers. Buckle your seatbelts, the ride is about to get extremely scenic and exciting!

1. Read Colossians 1:12-14. If you ever feel like life is hard and there is not much to be thankful for, the list provided in these verses will forever change your mind. Write out the 8 specific facts in these verses:

    1) v.12

    2) v.12

    3) v.12

    4) v.12

    5) v.13

    6) v.13

    7) v.14

    8) v.14

2. Colossians 1:13 states we are not only delivered from the power of darkness, we are **conveyed**, or transferred to a new location, the kingdom of the Son of His love. Read what Jesus had to say about darkness and light in Luke 11: 33-36 and write a summary contrasting the two.

3. Spend some time meditating on Colossians 1:14. Write out the 2 salvation phrases in this verse and tell what they mean to you. How do you define them (use other verses if you'd like)? Use your personal story to expound on the 2 phrases. Tell why and how the truth of this verse is a foundational reason to 'living happy'.

## Day Two

Are you ready for a profound theology lesson about your Savior? Read Colossians 1:15-18 several times and answer the following questions:

1. Using the verses you just read, list 10 facts that describe Jesus:

   1) v.15:

   2) v.15:

   3) v.16:

   4) v.16:

   5) v.17:

   6) v.17:

   7) v.18:

   8) v.18:

   9) v.18:

   10) v.18:

2. Now let's dig a little deeper and discover how other Scriptures confirm Paul's list. Look up each verse and write out the key words or phrases that provide greater clarity to who Jesus is:
   - Hebrews 1:2-3:

   - Psalm 89:4 & 27:

   - Hebrews 2:10:

   - John 1:1-3:

   - John 17:5:

   - Ephesians 1:22:

   - Revelation 1:5:

   - Isaiah 55:4:

   - 1Corinthians 15:20:

   - Psalm 2:7:

   - Acts 2:24:


From your study in the Scriptures today, spend some time using what you have written to offer up personal prayers of thanks and praise to God for His indescribable gift to you!

# The Surpassing Greatness of Jesus
## Day Three

1. Read Colossians 1:18 and write out the verse here:

2. Look up the word *preeminence* in the dictionary and write out the meaning here:

3. Even though the word *preeminence* is used nowhere else in the Bible, the concept is woven throughout Scripture. Look up the following verses and describe the preeminence of Christ in each one:
   - Ephesians 1:22-23:

   - Revelation 1:5:

   - John 14:6:

4. From this brief study, tell how the preeminence of Jesus makes a difference in your daily life. In other words, how does this Biblical truth impact the way you live?

5. How does the truth of Jesus' preeminence guarantee happiness for the believer?

**Day Four**
**Colossians 1: 19-23 is really the gospel in a nutshell.**

Read this portion of Scripture and answer the following questions:
1. Cross-reference John 1:16 and Colossians 2:9 to give a greater explanation of the 'fullness of Christ'.




2. Since Jesus is God in all of His fullness and totality, He is able to do what no mere man could ever do: reconcile sinners to a Holy God.
    List out all the things Jesus accomplished through His death on the cross that are revealed in v. 20-22:




3. Connect 2 Corinthians 5: 18-21 to Colossians 1:20-22 and show how Jesus has made peace for us. Tell how these truths are foundational to our freedom in Christ and how they enable us to 'live happy'.




4. Verse 23 gives some very practical advice for the believer. Explain how you stay grounded and steadfast in your hope.

**Day Five**
**Read Colossians 1:24-29**

Paul rejoiced in his sufferings. He saw this as taking his turn to suffer for the sake of the church. It was as if Paul was saying, 'how much will God let me put into it' rather than, 'what's in it for me?'

1. Read these additional scriptures and write down what you learn about suffering from each one:

   - Acts 5:41:

   - Matthew 5:10-12:

   - 1Peter 4:15-16:

2. Paul was the chosen apostle to the Gentiles. Read his expanded testimony in Ephesians 3:1-13 and write out any new insights you get into Paul's attitude towards the church and God's call on his life:

3. How do you respond when difficult things come your way? What can we learn from Paul's response? How do you think he was able to rejoice in his sufferings based on your study of Colossians so far?

4. What are the 3 things Paul said we are to do in our sharing of the Gospel according to verse 28?




5. As we come to the end of chapter one, use 1 Thessalonians 2:13 along with the Greek words for ***working*** and ***effectively*** to explain the balance between Paul's hard work and God's work:


**Greek words and definitions:**

**Working**-*energeia*-Strong's #1753: working, action, operative power. The English word 'energy' comes from this word. *Energeia* usually describes the working of God....

**Effectively**-*energeo*-Strong's #1754: One of the four big energy words: *energeo, energes, energeia*, and *energema*. The words all stem from ... "work" and have to do with the active operation or working of power and its effectual results.

(Hayford, Jack W. *New Spirit Filled Life Bible*. Nashville, TN: Thomas Nelson Bibles, 2002. 1673, 1685.Print)

# LIVE HAPPY
## – WEEK THREE –

Happiness is an inside job.

Day One
## Colossians 2

Colosse was one of three cities located about 100 miles inland from the major port city of Ephesus. The other two cities were Laodicea and Hierapolis (note Colossians 2:1 and 4:13 & 16). Paul spent 3 years ministering in Ephesus and then he left the church there under the care of Timothy, the man he had personally discipled. This tri-city area was a type of east-meets-west convergence zone because an important trade route passed through them. All kinds of religions and philosophies mingled together in this large cosmopolitan area.

In Colossians 2:1 Paul shared that he had a 'great conflict' for the people of this area. If you review the last few questions from last week, Paul shared that he was agonizing over these people in prayer, to the point of exhaustion. Paul knew, even though he had never been to Colosse, the people there needed specific instruction and encouragement to press in to Jesus, the true wisdom, the Author and Finisher of our faith. His earnest desire and spiritual longing for them was to cling to Jesus only and to make Him Lord of all.

Read Colossians 2:1-10 and answer the following questions:

1. In verses 2-3, Paul outlines another power-packed way we can pray for others. Write out the 5 specifics here:

2. How can living the way Paul instructed us to pray in these verses result in maintaining a happy life?

3. In verses 4-5 Paul gives a warning about the possibility of being deceived. What potential traps or deceptions are threatening Christians today?

4. What can you do personally to guard yourself against the snares or traps of the enemy/world?

5. How can you specifically help other believers to advance spiritually or to make spiritual progress? Use Hebrews 6:1 to help you answer.

## Book Note:

In his book, *The Invested Life,* author Joel Rosenberg says this: "God offers you eternal life. He wants you to live an abundant life. He calls you to the invested life. Every follower of Jesus Christ should be able to answer two simple questions: *Who is investing in me? Whom am I investing in?* God desires to pour an abundance of spiritual and emotional capital into your life....and he wants to use you to pour spiritual and emotional capital into the lives of others. Along the way, you'll be changed. Others will change. You'll grow. Others will grow. You'll feel loved. Others will feel loved. You will experience God and his community in a new and personal and supernatural way. And so will others."

(Rosenberg, Joel C., and T. E. Koshy, *The Invested Life: Making Disciples of Al Nations One Person at a time.* Carol Stream, IL, Tyndale House, 2012. 1. Print.)

**Day Two**
**Read Colossians 2:1-10**

1. In verse 6, Paul gives very practical advice for the believer. What does it mean for us to 'walk' in Christ? Be specific.

2. In verse 7, Paul gives 4 ways that we can 'live happy' in Jesus. List them here:

3. Using Ephesians 2:20-22, expand on what it means to be rooted and built up in Jesus.

4. In verse 7, Paul says our thanksgiving is to be _____. What does that mean to you in practical terms? How do you practice this kind of thanksgiving?

**Day Three**
**Read Colossians 2:6-10**

## Book Note:

In his book, *The Happiness Advantage*, author Shawn Achor highlights the benefits of gratitude: "When our brains constantly scan for and focus on the positive, we profit from three of the most important tools available to us: happiness, gratitude, and optimism. Studies have shown that consistently grateful people are more energetic, emotionally intelligent, forgiving and less likely to be depressed, anxious or lonely. And it's not that people are only grateful because they are happier either; gratitude has proven to be a significant cause of positive outcomes. When researchers pick random volunteers and train them to be more grateful over a period of a few weeks, they become happier and more optimistic, feel more socially connected, enjoy better quality sleep, and even experience fewer headaches than control groups."

(Achor, Shawn. *The Happiness Advantage: The Seven Principles of Positive Psychology That Fuel Success and Performance at Work.* New York: Crown Business. 2010. 97-98. Print.)

1. Write out a few things you are thankful for in regards to your faith in Jesus.

2. What are the 4 things we are to avoid or beware of in verse 8?

3. From your list in question 4, give a definition of each one and a practical example of each one.

4. In verses 9 & 10, Paul gives the counter-offensive to verse 8. What are the three absolute truths about Jesus that Paul states in these verses:

5. Other verses in the Bible echo these truths. Look up the following passages and write out the facts from each verse and tell how this impacts your daily life:
    - Ephesians 3:19:

    - Ephesians 1:20-21:

    - 1Peter 3:22:

    - Psalm 110:1:

**Day Four**
**Read Colossians 2: 11-15**
Circumcision was required for the Jewish people as a sign of the covenant between God and Abraham. This external act symbolized how Abraham and all of his descendants were God's covenant people. Circumcision showed that their confidence was placed in the promises of God and His faithfulness, not the flesh.

1. Paul felt the need to bring up circumcision as it related to the believer's identity. Why do you think this was significant? Use Deuteronomy 10:16 and 30:6; Romans 2:28-29; 3:30; 4:9-10 and 15:8 to formulate an explanation.

2. Now the outward sign believers participate in is _____ (v. 12). What are the two verbs used by Paul in this verse that give meaning to this symbolic sign?

3. Have you been baptized as a sign and symbol of your faith and relationship with Jesus? If not, prayerfully talk this over with Him.

**Day Five**
**Read Colossians 2: 13-15**
1. List the 8 things Jesus accomplished through His death on the cross for us according to these verses. Then spend some time thanking God for each one as an act of worship.

2. Read the prophetic account of what Jesus endured for us in Isaiah 53. What do you love about this story? What comforts, encourages, and challenges you about it?

# LIVEHAPPY
## – WEEK FOUR –

Now and then it's good to pause in our pursuit of happiness and just be happy.

~ G. APOLLINAIRE ~

**Day One**
**Read Colossians 2:16-23**

Have you ever felt judged by other Christians?

This section in Paul's letter deals heavily with legalism and religious practice. Many beliefs, other than Jesus and His finished work on the cross, were infiltrating the church at Colosse. Paul sought to deal with these false beliefs with a resounding blow. In light of all we just studied last time regarding the accomplishments of Jesus' death, burial, and resurrection, let's study and discover how we can prevent becoming victims of legalism.

### Greek word and definition:

**Judge**: *krino;* Strong's #2919: To separate, decide, examine, question, select, choose, resolve, make an opinion, determine, decide favorably or unfavorably, pronounce judgment.

(Hayford, Jack W. *New Spirit Filled Life Bible.* Nashville, TN: Thomas Nelson Bibles, 2002. 1476. Print.)

1. According to Acts 15:10 & Galatians 5:1, how should we respond to the Law?

2. Read Galatians 3:24-4:7 and summarize what these Scriptures teach about the Law.

3. Who does the Law reveal, according to Luke 24:27?

4. What does Hebrews 10:1 say about the Law?

5. Look up the following verses and explain how we get to come to God:
   - Hebrews 4:16:

   - Hebrews 10:19:

   - John 14:6:

   - 1Timothy 2:5:

**Day Two**
**Read Colossians 2: 16-23**
Paul encouraged believers to *'hold fast to the Head'*. In other words, press in to Jesus; hold on to Him. We are inadequate for a single day without Him at the center of our lives.

1. What do the following verses reveal about the Body of Christ?
   - Romans 12:4:

   - Ephesians 4:4-16:

   - 1 Corinthians 12:12-13:

2. Asceticism is the practice of rigorous self-denial and self-mortification in order to become more spiritual. What do you learn from 1Timothy 4:1-5 in regards to self-denial and the *'don't do's'* of life?

3. What is the balance the Bible provides for us as seen in these verses?
   - 1Timothy 4:3 & 8:

   - 1Corinthians 9:27:

   - 1Timothy 6:17:

   - Mark 7:18:

   - Romans 14:14:

## Book Note:

In their book, *Intuitive Eating,* authors Tribole and Resch, encourage people to make peace with food and to get free from chronic dieting, or the do's and don'ts of eating:

"Get rid of the *musts, oughts, shoulds, need tos, supposed tos,* and *have tos.* Every time you think that you must go on a diet, or you need to lose ten pounds before the reunion, or you ought to have a light lunch like a salad and tea, or you shouldn't eat before you go to bed, stop yourself and replace those thoughts.

Each time that you think in exaggerated ways, you create miserable feelings for yourself, and, once again, compensate by extreme behaviors. The following are examples of catastrophic thoughts:

- I'll never be thin.
- It's hopeless.
- I'll never get a boyfriend or a job at this weight.
- My life is ruined because I'm so fat.
- If I let myself eat candy bars and fries, I'll eat them forever.

This kind of thinking is a real setup…You tell yourself that all your happiness hinges on your eating and your body."

(Tribole, Evelyn, and Elyse Resch. *Intuitive Eating.* New York: St. Martin's Griffin, 2012. 116-117. Print.)

**Day Three**
**Read Colossians 2: 16-23**

1. Summarize what you have learned so far from your study of this portion of Paul's letter. *For personal reflection: Is Jesus preeminent in your life, or are you relying on some other man-made religious rule, system or substitute?*

2. If you were having a conversation with a legalist, how would you explain verse 23 to them? Put this verse in your own words.

3. What does the Christian have according to 2 Peter 1:4?

4. Look up John 4:24 and explain how believers are to worship and tell how this relates to legalism.

## Day Four
# Colossians Three
**Read Colossians 3:1-11**

In these last 2 chapters of Colossians, Paul shifts his instruction to the practical application of the theology and doctrines he had been teaching. Paul desired the believers of his day to truly understand what it meant to live as Christians. It's one thing to *defend* the truth, but Christ-followers must also *demonstrate* it in their daily lives. Our lives are meant to reveal our message. Jesus taught us that others would know we are Christians by our love—not just love for others, but also love for Him, so that our lives honor Him and point others to Him.

The pagan religions of Paul's day did not teach on personal holiness. Worshippers could bow before an idol or leave their gifts at the altar and not change a thing about the way they lived. When Christianity came on to the scene, the pagan world began to see people whose beliefs were backed up by their behavior. It's important to understand the order of things: our beliefs directly impact our behavior.

1. Verses 1, 3 and 4 tell us about our identity and position in Christ. Understanding and embracing these truths enable us to live out what we believe. Write the four things these verses reveal about our *current* Christ-centered position:

2. Read Ephesians 2:4-7 and list out in greater detail our position and standing in Christ:

3. Verse two is another practical instruction from Paul. Jesus Himself taught on this principle. Read Matthew 6:19-21 and explain how Jesus' teachings and Paul's instruction are the same.

4. Verse three is a critical verse for every believer to understand and embrace. Write out verse three here:

5. Look up the following verses and write the key phrases that tie in to verse three:

  - Galatians 2:20:

  - Romans 6:2:

  - 2 Corinthians 5:14:

**Day Five**
**Read Colossians 3:1-4**

1. Paul makes an amazing statement in verse 4 when he tells us that *'Christ is our life'*. What does this phrase mean to you? How would you practically explain this to a new Christian or a pre-believer who is seeking answers to life?

2. For more insight into this concept stated in verse 4, look up 1John 3:2 and John 14:6 and write out a more expanded view of Paul's statement using these verses:

3. When Christ is our life, this enables us to truly *'live happy'*. Take the rest of today's study time to write out your personal prayer of praise and thanks to Jesus for His all-encompassing, life-changing power and Presence in your life!

# LIVEHAPPY
## – WEEK FIVE –

It's not how much we have, but how much we enjoy, that makes happiness.

~ CHARLES SPURGEON ~

# Living for Jesus
Day One

As we mentioned last week, Colossians 3 and 4 are the practical out-working of the doctrines Paul taught. Sometimes, one of the most practical things we can do is make a list! The next few sections of the Scripture we study will involve some list-making. It does feel satisfying when we have a long to-do list (can you say Christmas shopping?!) and we get to cross things off!

**Book Note:**

In her book, *The Happiness Project,* Gretchen Rubin shares a light-hearted list that she calls "The Secrets of Adulthood":

- People don't notice your mistakes as much as you think.
- It's okay to ask for help.
- Most decisions don't require extensive research.
- It's important to be nice to everyone.
- Bring a sweater.
- By doing a little each day, you can get a lot accomplished.
- Soap and water remove most stains.
- If you can't find something, clean up.
- You can choose what you do; you can't choose what you *like* to do.
- What you do *every day* matters more than what you do *once in a while*.
- You can't profoundly change your children's natures by nagging them or signing them up for classes.
- No deposit, no return.

(Rubin, Gretchen Craft. *The Happiness Project: Or Why I Spent a Year Trying to Sing in the Morning, Clean My Closets, Fight Right, Read Aristotle, and Generally Have More Fun.* New York: HarperCollins, 2009, 11. Print.)

**Read Colossians 3: 5-11**

From your reading, answer the following questions:

1. In verse 5, Paul tells us there are certain things we are to 'put to death'. What does it mean to 'put to death' things in our lives?

2. Make a list of the things from Paul in verse 5, and put them into a vernacular anyone could understand or relate to:

3. Use the following verses to explain the concept of 'putting to death' the things in our lives that are contrary to the love of Christ:
    - Romans 6:13:
    - Romans 8:13:
    - Matthew 15:19:
    - 2Timothy 2:22:
    - Ephesians 5:3:

Finish today's time in the Word by praying over the things you've studied, and ask the Holy Spirit to reveal anything in your life that needs to be 'put to death'.

**Day Two**
**Read Colossians 3:5-11**

1. Verse 6 talks about that 'hellfire and brimstone' topic: the wrath of God. In today's world, most people like to avoid this topic, however, Paul found it extremely important to discuss. Who does Paul tell us the wrath of God is coming upon?

    - Read Romans 1:18. Where is the wrath of God revealed from and who receives it?
    - Read Ephesians 5:6-7. What is the specific instruction in these verses regarding the wrath of God?

2. In verses 7 & 8, Paul is talking directly to us. He uses the term, *'you yourselves'*. What did he say we used to do? What are we now to do? (Make your list!)

3. It's one thing to make a list, it's another thing to carry it out. Look up Ephesians 4:21-24 for some spiritually helpful ways to carry out the instructions to *'put off'*. The first one is done for you:
    - Hear Christ and be taught by Him v. 21
    - 
    -

4. From your brief study today, write out some practical ways we can obey the biblical commands of verses 5-8. It's important to be mindful of being *spiritually* practical while being careful not to become legalistic in our desire to obey the commands here. (For example: Renewing my mind by reading my Bible daily will equip me in my battle against coveting.)

5. How can *putting to death* or *putting off* these things contribute to living a happy life?

**Day Three**
**Read Colossians 3:9-11**

1. In verse 9, we see that our words are so important to God, why do you think this is so?

2. Answer the following questions:
   - According to John 8:44, who is the liar?

   - Look up John 14:17 & 15:26. Who is the Spirit of truth?

   - Read Ephesians 4:25-27. How do these verses relate to our words?

3. Verse 10 reveals that we are going someplace! We are either making spiritual progress and being renewed in our minds, or we are going backwards. What do these verses teach us about practical renewal?
   - Romans 12:2:

   - 2 Corinthians 4:16:

   - Ephesians 4:23:

   - 2 Corinthians 3:18:

   - John 8:31-32:

4. Verse 11 is a beautiful statement on unity. In Paul's day, a Barbarian was a person who neither spoke Greek nor embraced Greek culture. Scythians were a lower caste of people among the Barbarians. Paul stressed to all believers that there is no room for disunity in the body of Christ, no matter who is involved. What do these two passages teach us about unity?

- Romans 10:12:

- Galatians 3:26-28:

5. As a benediction to these profound principles in living out our Christianity with our words, daily renewal, and actions towards others, read 1 Corinthians 13:1-13, the famous *'love chapter'* and list all the things love is and love is not.

Prayerfully consider this passage in light of your current relationships with others. What are some evidences of Christian unity that you have personally seen and experienced? Be sure and thank God for that!

**Day Four**
**Read Colossians 3:12-17**
**It's list-making time again...**

1. Review Colossians 3:8 and compare this verse with Colossians 3:12. Make a contrasting list showing what we are to put off and put on:

2. Bearing with others and forgiving them is sometimes the hardest thing to do in life. Paul knew this, so he was sure to include it here! List out the principle of forgiveness from each of the following verses:

    - Mark 11:25:

    - Luke 23:34:

    - Colossians 1:14:

    - Ephesians 4:32:

    - Matthew 6:14:

    - Acts 4:12:

3. What did you learn from question 2? How's your heart? Is there anyone in your life you need to follow up with to set things right?

4. How does forgiving others enable us to live happy? Spend time reflecting on the verses from today, asking God to renew your mind by them. Use the space below to journal your thoughts and prayers.

**Day Five**
**Read Colossians 3:12-17**

Greek word and definition:

**Forgiving,** *charizomai; Strong's;* #5483: To do a favor, show kindness unconditionally, give freely, grant forgiveness, forgive freely. The word is from the same root as *charis,* "grace."

"Forgiveness is made possible through Christ, who forgave us. It is an act in which one person releases another from an offense…. To forgive is not to condone the sin as acceptable, to say it made no difference, or to license repetition of it. Rather, forgiveness is a choice…."

(Hayford, Jack W. *New Spirit Filled Life Bible.* Nashville, TN: Thomas Nelson Bibles, 2002. 1675. Print.)

1. What does Matthew 18:15-35 teach us about the Christ-like process we are to walk through when we have an offense with another? Summarize and write out the principles.

2. Paul made it clear in verse 14 that love is the most important thing we are to *put on*. What do you learn about love from the following verses?

    - 1 Peter 4:8:

    - Proverbs 10:12:

    - Proverbs 17:9:

    - Colossians 1:8:


3. How does love, the most important thing we are to put on, impact forgiveness and bearing with one another? Why is cultivating love the most pro-active thing we can do in our walks with the Lord?

# LIVE HAPPY
## – WEEK SIX –

Most people are
as happy as they
make up their
minds to be.

~ ABRAHAM LINCOLN ~

## Living a life of gratitude
**Day One**

The journey through Colossians 3 has taken us a while and we still have a way to go! These verses have been power-packed with the preeminence of Christ. When Jesus is the center of our lives, we learn what to *put on* and *put off*. We learn the value of speaking truthfully, loving our brothers and sisters in Christ, and forgiving others when offenses come our way. This week, everything comes closer to home as we dig deeper into what it means for Jesus to be preeminent in our families and the workplace. My prayer is that we all enjoy the ride!

**Read Colossians 3:14-17**

1. What are the two commands given to us in verse 15?

2. Do you think peace and thankfulness are connected to each other? Why or why not?

3. How would thankfulness facilitate greater peace in our lives? <u>**Try this:**</u> Find 20 things/people around your home and life you are thankful for and take a picture of them on your smart phone. Scroll through these pictures once a day this week and give thanks out loud to God for each one!

*"The demands of Jesus are only as hard to obey as His promises are hard to cherish and His Presence is hard to treasure."*

~Pastor and author, John Piper

**Day Two**
**Read Colossians 3: 16-17**

1. List the positive things we are commanded to do in verse 16:

2. How does verse 16 contribute to living happy? What does this look like in *your* life?

3. What is your current favorite *'spiritual song'*? Spend some time today worshiping God with your favorite praise music.

4. Read the following entry provided by author and songwriter, Mary Nystrom:

> "Let the word of Christ dwell in you richly in all wisdom,
>
> teaching and admonishing one another
>
> in psalms and hymns and spiritual songs,
>
> singing with grace in your hearts to the Lord."
>
> Colossians 3:16 NKJV

We made it! After 3,000 highway miles across twelve states, a string of mom and pop motels, and disappointing roadside attractions, our weary family arrived at the Long Island home of beloved friends.

Before I could turn off the van's ignition, the front door of the house flew open and out rolled a long red remnant purchased at a local carpet store. Though frayed on the edges and not perfectly rectangular, the bright crimson pathway boldly proclaimed, "We've been expecting you! Come on in! Make yourself at home!"

I thought of this experience as I studied the opening phrase of Colossians 3:16, "Let the word of Christ dwell in you richly..." It speaks of the red-carpet welcome we should give to the words of Jesus—and to the entire Word of God.

The word "dwell" is from the Greek word *enoikeo*. This is a compound word formed from *en* (in) and *oikos* (house) and paints the image of someone firmly settled in a home. Here "richly" is the translation of *plousios*—a Greek word denoting great wealth and prosperity. Taken together, the word pair conveys we are made spiritual millionaires as we open up and let God's Word pervade every corner of our lives. A wealth of wisdom is gained as we allow scripture to makes its home in our minds and hearts.

The second half of Colossians 3:16 lists some of the benefits of a life saturated with the living Word of God. As we are enriched by spiritual insight there is a natural overflow that encourages others in their faith— "teaching and admonishing one another..."

There is something in nature biologists call symbiosis. This happens when two species, plant or animal, receive mutual benefit from interaction with one another. An example is the relationship between the clownfish and the sea anemone. Immune from its venom, the small fish finds refuge among the anemone's stinging tentacles. In turn, its vivid orange color is a tantalizing lure, drawing larger prey toward the anemone's mouth.

Scripture and music enjoy a symbiotic relationship. They too enliven and enhance one another. For centuries the truths of the Bible have inspired song – from David's psalms to Handel's Messiah, from a child's spontaneous praises to the contemporary worship of today's churches. Song is a natural outflow of a heart impacted by God's Word.

On the other hand, melody helps us express and memorize scripture. Through the ages the hymns of the church have both exalted God and taught Biblical lessons. Martin Luther called music "the handmaiden of theology" for its power to transmit and solidify biblical truth in the worshiper. Many of the verses I have committed to memory were learned as a scripture chorus.

In Colossians 3:16 Paul shows us how the scripture/music relationship worked in the early church. He lists a complete three-course meal of song – each needed for its unique and specific role in releasing heart-felt worship.

- **Psalms:** This refers to the Book of Psalms. These were written to be sung, not merely spoken. Several of the psalms begin with an introduction that gives specific musical direction such as, "to be sung to the tune 'Lilies'" (Psalm 69). The psalms are often quoted in the New Testament – perhaps because the writers could recall the lyrics of these familiar songs. The psalms of David show us that our worship can express the whole gamut of human emotion – from the depths of despair to the heights of spiritual elation.

- **Hymns:** Most scholars agree the term "hymns" refers to songs of human composition that, though not verbatim scripture, contain lyrics of praise to God and/or instruction in theology.

- **Spiritual songs:** The phrase "spiritual song" comes from two Greek words, *pneumatikos* and *ode* respectively. It's easy to see the English word "ode" has its origin in Greek i.e. Ode to Joy or Ode to Bill Joe. It simply means "song." The word *pneumatikos* translated "spiritual" comes from the root work *pneuma,* which means "breath." Many believe a true spiritual song is a "spirit-breathed" song, unpremeditated and unrehearsed—a brand new song that spontaneously flows from the heart and mouth of an honest and unrestrained worshiper. We find examples of spontaneous song in the lives of Bible characters including Moses, Miriam, Hannah, David, and Mary.

Today, many worshipers include hymns and scripture-based choruses in their times of corporate or personal devotion. Sadly, the third member of the Colossians 3:16 trinity, spiritual song, is usually ignored. For most of us, the idea of singing out loud is frightening enough – the idea of ad-libbing brand new lyrics is horrifying.

Small children, untainted by the jeers of peers or the remarks of Simon Cowell, find it enjoyable and natural to sing out spontaneous songs about whatever is on their mind. My son, Nathan, put Seahawk scores and stats to melody when he was young. Unfortunately, as we get older, this God-given inclination to sing impromptu songs is easily stifled and shut down by peers, contemporary culture, and our own feelings of inadequacy.

Consequently, we miss out on developing this part of the three-fold expression of worship encouraged by Paul in Colossians 3:16. I believe spiritual songs are one of the most enriching forms of worship. Let me encourage you to find a private place to develop the discipline of spiritual song in your daily communion with God. It will enrich and broaden your worship of Jesus.

Here are some important benefits of including spiritual song in your personal devotions:

- **Scripture songs:** Open the Bible and sing your own melodies to favorite verses. The addition of rhythm and pitches can often make scripture come alive and easier to recall.

- **Prayer songs:** Every form of prayer – supplication, intercession, or confessions, can be empowered with song. St. Augustine famously said, "He who sings prays twice." We wouldn't have the Psalms today if its writers hadn't recorded the wide variety of their prayer songs.

- **Personalized songs:** As much as we love the grandeur of hymns and the poetic lyrics of worship choruses, they don't always meet us "where we're at." God loves honest worship. He doesn't fall off His throne when we "tell it like it is." David didn't hold back when he poured out his thoughts, feelings, questions, and complaints in song. Honesty incites intimacy.

- **Thanksgiving songs:** There is no greater song of gratitude than one that recounts specific blessings from the hand of God. When we create our own lyrics we can include the names of family members and friends, material provision, and the many, many ways God is uniquely working in our lives.

- **Spiritual warfare songs:** Free-flowing and sincere worship is one of our most potent weapons in our spiritual arsenal. The enemy of our soul and his influence on our thoughts dissipate as sincere worship rises.

Many choruses now sung by church congregations began as a spiritual song in the writer's quiet time or in a corporate gathering. Laurie Klein's worship classic, "I Love You, Lord", was birthed as she sang a spontaneous song to Jesus while washing dishes at the kitchen sink. God may use you to write a song—whether it be for Jesus alone, your local church, or worshipers around the globe.

**Day Three**
**Read Colossians 3:17**

1. How do we practically live out the directive given to us in this verse?

2. Cross-reference 1Corinthians 10:31 with verse 17 and write out an expanded meaning of this directive.

3. How does thanksgiving practically tie-in with the lifestyle expressed in this verse?

4. The preeminence of Jesus is seen in 4 spiritual motivations for living a life that reveals Him. Review the following verses and list out these motivations:
- Colossians 3:11:

- Colossians 3:13:

- Colossians 3:15:

- Colossians 3:16:

**Day Four**
**Read Colossians 3: 18-25**

1. Separate out each group of people addressed in verses 18-22. Next to each group, write down:
   1) **What** were they directed to do.
   2) The reason **why** they were directed to do it.
   3) How the preeminence of Christ impacts the **what** and the **why**?

2. Where do you fit into this list? Which of the directives apply to you? What do you personally glean from this part of Paul's letter? Is there anything you have trouble with in this passage?

3. Read the following entry and afterwards spend some time praying about what you have read and journal any new insights you glean from your reading.

**A Father's Perspective:**

***Colossians 3:21 – Fathers, do not provoke your children, lest they become discouraged.***

Commonplace is the ability to see the negative in another person. And, because familiarity breeds contempt, with 20/20 vision we are so capable of seeing the faults of our family members. Thus is the predicament we find ourselves in with our children. Our daughter comes home with a report card of all A's and one B. What do we see, and what do we say? My son gets thrown out at second trying to stretch a single into a double. What do we see, and what do we say? Do I see an opportunity to speak to a positive character quality displayed in such an effort, or do I find fault in his ill-fated attempt? Indeed, "death and life are in the power of the tongue, and those who love it will eat its fruit" (Proverbs 18:21). So why is ongoing discouragement such a harmful experience for a child?

Courage is the virtue by which all other virtues are built upon. Without courage, sacrificial and selfless Christian living has no mooring and cannot be maintained. C. S. Lewis put it this way, "Courage is not simply one of the virtues, but the form of every virtue at the testing point." We want our children to be brave: To "be strong and very courageous" (Joshua 1:7). But where does courage come from? It comes from encouragement. When we encourage our children, we build courage into them. When we discourage them, we take away their ability to amass the virtues of bravery and courage. Children who are consistently encouraged by their fathers and mothers throughout childhood will be the ones able to go up against and slay the many giants we know they will face in adulthood.

So why ought we to encourage our children? Because God is constantly encouraging us through His Word! Each and every day we wake up to His Word speaking to us once again, telling us He will never leave us nor forsake us; He accepts us in the Beloved; there is no condemnation in Christ Jesus our Lord; every promise is yes and amen; and we can do all things through Christ who strengthens us. If God the Father is the source and well-spring of all encouragement to us as parents, why would we not pass that on to our children? If He is constantly pointing out my new-found identity I have in Jesus Christ, why would I not pass along that same standing to my children? While there will always be opportunities to correct and admonish our children, let it be done in such a way that builds up versus tear down, and may it always be greatly counter-weighted by words of life, the same words we receive each day by our Heavenly Father.

~Special Thanks to Steve Schaefer for this entry

**Day Five**
**Read Colossians 3: 22-4: 1**

Slavery was an established institution in Paul's day. Many slaves were highly educated and held great responsibilities in the homes of the wealthy. The first-century church did not openly oppose slavery or seek to destroy it because the church was a minority group that had no political power to change an institution that was built on the social order of the day. Paul was careful to instruct Christian slaves to secure their freedom if they could (read 1Corinthians 7:21), but he did not encourage rebellion or the overthrow of the existing order.

Also remember the book of Colossians was a letter written while Paul was imprisoned in a Roman cell. The book of Philemon was another letter written from his cell which also reveals his attitude towards slavery (more on that in the next chapter). A Christian slave was expected to obey his master as a ministry to the Lord.

(Wiersbe, Warren W. *The Wiersbe Bible Commentary.* Colorado Springs: David C. Cook, 2007. 691. Print.)

1. What were the specific commands given to '*bondservants*' and why was this important?

2. Verse 23 echoes Colossians 3:17. What does it mean to do something *heartily?* Look up Ecclesiastes 9:10 and Romans 12:11 to help you answer.

3. What is the motivation found in verse 24?

**Greek word and definition:**

**Partiality,** *prosopolepsia;* Strong's #4382: Favoritism, partiality, distinction, bias, conditional preference.  The word denotes a biased judgment, which gives respect to rank, position, or circumstances instead of considering the intrinsic conditions.  God shows no partiality in justice, judgment, or favorable treatment when dealing with people, and He expects us to follow His example.

(Hayford, Jack W. *New Spirit Filled Life Bible*. Nashville, TN: Thomas Nelson Bibles, 2002. 1676. Print.)


4. Using this Greek definition of the word *partiality,* tell how and why maintaining the preeminence of Christ in our lives would prevent us from having a bias towards others in the workplace and in life in general.

# LIVE HAPPY
## – WEEK SEVEN –

One of the sanest, surest, and most encompassing joys of life comes from being happy over the good works and good fortune of others.

~ ARCHIBALD RUTLEDGE ~

# At home and at work
## Day One
A word to modern-day *"bondservants"* ....

### Colossians 3:22-4:1 – Bondservants and Masters

Work is war. The workplace a battlefield. The warfare of deadlines, agendas, co-workers, bosses, complaint, lack of integrity, lies, back-stabbing, fears, pressures, stress, layoffs, and pay-cuts. Sound like fun? This spiritual, emotional, and mental war can leave us physically worn out and feeling beat up. But what if you really like your job? You are not immune. The land mines of authority, power and the love of money can draw you away from your first love, leaving some to "wander from the faith."

So if this is a war, how should we approach it? How should we head into each work day, and what is the spirit we ought to head in with? The answers are found in 2 Chronicles 20. With the invading armies of Ammon, Moab, and Mount Seir about to attack, Judah was in an impossible situation. Completely outnumbered, Jehoshaphat and the people he ruled were about to be completely obliterated. Realizing the battle is the Lord's, Jehoshaphat sets himself to seek the Lord, concluding his prayer with the humble dependence of "we know not what to do but our eyes are upon You." And the Lord's response? "Do not be afraid nor dismayed because of this great multitude, for the battle is not yours, but God's". Jehoshaphat's confidence came not from his own ingenuity, skills, or talents, but because of the Lord's presence: "Do not fear or be dismayed; tomorrow go out against them, for the Lord is with you." With this confidence, who goes before the army of the Lord into battle? The Marines? No, it was the praise and worship singers:

> *"And when he had consulted with the people, he appointed those who should sing to the Lord, and who should praise the beauty of His holiness, as they went out before the army and were saying: Praise the Lord, for His mercy endures forever. Now when they began to sing and to praise, the Lord set ambushes of Ammon, Moab, and Mount Seir, who had come against Judah; and they were defeated."* 2Chronicles 20: 21 NKJV

Praise led the way. Praise because they knew they had the victory. They went into battle knowing the end from the beginning. And so it is with us: We win, so praise leads the way. Having the promises and practicing His presence, we go to work each day not knowing what to do but having our eyes on Him. Thus the praising and worshiping Christian at work is joyful, grateful, and **happy**. We see the glass half full, assume the best, and treat others innocent until proven guilty. Walking in the victory that is ours, we have fun and can laugh and show humor while in the midst of the war we are engaged in.

So praise your Savior! Worship Him on the way in, and thank Him in advance for the victory His own hand has secured for you. In Christ, we have the victory, so let's play to win through our praise and worship of Him!

~Thanks to Steve Schaefer for this perspective on the Christian in the workplace

1. What did you learn from the Scripture and this entry on having a preeminent view of Christ in the workplace?

2. Spend the rest of your study time today praying about what you have read and studied. If you are currently employed outside of the home, spend extended time praying about your job and for your fellow employees and those in authority over you.

   If this particular piece in Colossians does not apply to you directly, pray for those you know who are employed, or those looking for a job, or pray for your husband and his job situation.

**Day Two**
**Read Colossians 4:2-6**

1. What did Jesus teach about prayer in Luke 18:1? How does this parallel what Paul teaches in verse 2?

2. After spending his entire letter instructing the church at Colosse, Paul asks for prayer himself. What are his main concerns he requests to be covered in prayer?

3. In these verses, Paul singles out 3 ingredients that should characterize our relationship to the unbelieving world. What are they?
    - Verses 2-4:
    - Verse 5:
    - Verse 6:

4. What does it mean to 'walk in wisdom' and to 'redeem the time'? Use Matthew 10:16 to help you answer.

5. What 3 things are important in our communication with others, according to verse 6?

6. Describe what graceful speech, seasoned with salt sounds like on a daily basis. (Use the themes of Colossians as you write your description: unity, love, acceptance, truth, etc.)

**Day Three**
**Read Colossians 4: 7-18**

We are coming to the end of our journey. This small letter has been full of transforming truth, principles, directives and encouragements. As we finish reading Paul's letter, it becomes obvious that he was very relational.

In these last few days of study, we come full circle. We see that Paul ends his letter the same way he began it: praying grace and peace upon the people and specifically encouraging others.

At the end of the day, the Christian life is really all about **relationships**. Our new life starts in relationship with Jesus and from there, every person we come in contact with has the opportunity to experience Christ in us—*hope of glory*.

When I was in college, I read a book that forever changed and impacted the way I related to people. It was an obscure book that most people have never heard of, but it is probably the most influential book in my life, next to the Bible itself.

Concentric Circles of Concern, by W. Oscar Thompson has this to say in chapter one: "The most important word in the English language, apart from proper nouns, is *relationship*. You say, but *love* has to be the most important word.

I ask you though, where is love going if there is no relationship? Relationship is the track. Love is what rolls over the track. Love moves through a relationship. *But the thing that satisfies the deepest longing of your being is a relationship with someone...*there is something built into people that desires to be wanted, to be needed, to be fulfilled. Those desires are fulfilled only in relationships. There are people in your spheres of influence---your concentric circles—whom you touch every day, and you do not even see them. Some of them are cantankerous, some of them you do not like, and some of them you really do not want to love; but they are there. They are there for you to love—to meet their needs—to draw to Jesus." (Thompson, W. Oscar. *Concentric Circles of Concern*. Nashville, TN: Broadman, 1981. 13+. Print.)

1. Count and list the names of the people Paul specifically mentions in this portion of the letter. If Paul gives a description, write that beside the name.

2. Onesimus (in verse 9) was most likely the same runaway slave mentioned in **the book of Philemon**. Take some time to read that short letter from Paul regarding this man, his relationship to Paul, and the significance of his story to the church in Colosse.

3. In Philemon 6, what is the result of the sharing of our faith?

4. What are some specific ways that you can *acknowledge every good thing which is in you in Christ Jesus?*

5. In Philemon 8-16, Paul once again is dishing out relationship advice! Write down the principles you see in these verses regarding forgiveness and restoration.

**Day Four**
**Continuing the relationship theme….**

If you did not finish all of the homework from yesterday's assignment, take some time to do that since today's assignment will be reading only.

### Book Note:

Today we hear a lot of buzz about *story*. And who doesn't like a good story? Stories help us remember things we learn and it makes learning so much more interesting.

A book was released late this summer that is a worthwhile read. Speak: How your story can change the world, by Nish Weiseth, is provocative and challenging. The following is an excerpt from the forward of the book by Shauna Niequist:

"Our culture specializes in boxes, in categories, in labels. We think we know everything there is to know about someone because they send their kids to this or that kind of school, or because they go to this or that kind of church, or because they have this or that kind of sticker on their car. This is sloppy. And this is dangerous.

And this is why story matters. Because when you listen to a story, you have to give up your stereotypes and your labels. Because stories crawl out of the boxes every chance they get. Because stories zig when we think they'll zag. Stories surprise us around every corner. Stories reach out and grab our labels and shred them to confetti." (Weiseth, Nish. *Speak: How Your Story Can Change the World.* Grand Rapids, MI: Zondervan, 2014. 13-14. Print.)

Grab a cup of coffee or tea and read the next two stories that reveal lives that have been impacted by the love of Christ and His transforming power.

## I Never Thought I'd Be Happy Again

When I went through my divorce, I was so broken hearted and wounded, I wasn't sure I would ever be happy again. I knew I would physically live through the divorce process, but felt that my truly joyful self was dead. I thought I would be one of those people that to be in my presence would reveal an unhealed, wounded soul resulting in a permanent barrier to happiness. I did not understand why God allowed my circumstances, however, I knew my hope was in my risen Savior and I had to trust God's Word – every verse, every promise without exception, regardless of what my eyes saw.

In the early dark days, I had this frequent, simple prayer of desperation, "Jesus, get the kids and I through this." At first, I found solace with the Psalmist who understood my grieving heart. After some time, I needed hope. My prayers began to change as I set my mind on things above.

When I saw a promise of God in the Bible, I'd say aloud, "You said Lord…., make it so in my life and my children's." And then it began: baby steps of radical change. Obstacles were being cast into the sea, and my faith was being built. The more I pressed into the Lord for His promises, provision and protection, the more I saw Him move.

After nearly two years, I was not cognizant of how much I had changed until one week when I had two nearly identical conversations, one with my mother and the other with my best friend from high school. At a point in each of the conversations, both individuals, stopped and exclaimed, "You're back!" I had no idea what they meant and asked for clarification. They told me that my old joyful self was alive and well.

As I pondered their words, I realized the barrier to my **happiness** had eroded due to my total dependence in my heavenly Father, what Christ did for me on the cross and the power of the Holy Spirit. I did not choose the path of divorce, but I did choose to *press into Jesus* who revealed His *complete fullness* in my circumstance. Today, I deeply abide in joy, and am eternally grateful that I am hidden in Christ, fully redeemed and secure in my salvation.

~Thank you, Vickie Adair, for sharing your story with us!

## A Long Road to Happiness

Most of us can relate to having blue days and sadness following a loss or disappointment. This is normal. But try to imagine living days, weeks, months or years where there is nothing in life that brings a smile, a laugh or pleasure of any kind. This is true, deep, clinical depression, and most people who have experienced it would describe it as something like a suffocating darkness that sucks you down relentlessly. This is my story.

Most people in deep depression would give anything for some relief and that's where thoughts of suicide come in. They believe, as I did, that everyone would be better off if I weren't here. This is where I lived off and on for twenty years following a head injury sustained in an auto accident. Following the accident, my personality changed completely and instantly. I had always been the happy, glass is half-full, can-do, morning person. Now I was suddenly moody, anxious, angry, sleepless, in constant pain, dealing with cognitive and memory problems, and overwhelmed by life.

By God's grace, we managed to keep functioning, but at a severely impaired state. Doctors gave no hope, either offering narcotics, anti-depressants (that didn't work), or saying I was mental and needed counseling.

Doctors finally diagnosed the traumatic brain injury at year 14. After the accident, my life became consumed by anxiety and fear. My physical health also began deteriorating rapidly in every area you could possibly imagine. I was inexplicably gaining weight at insane rates. I gained 105 pounds in 26 weeks over three separate events – 40 pounds in 8 weeks, then 45 in 12 weeks and then 20 in four weeks. But the biggest thing was the overwhelming, *suffocating depression* that I could not escape from. I felt my body was betraying me and I begged God to please let me die. I felt terrible guilt for what living with a severally depressed wife and mother was doing to my husband and daughters.

The church was a blessing because my family, especially my girls, had stability there. Worship was always a drink of water in my dry-desert life. I cried through every worship service I attended for years because I would feel God's presence and hear scriptures that I would cling to for dear life, literally.

I sometimes heard Pastors say things like "if you're depressed, get over it," or: "unrepented sin is the reason we have diseases like …," and "you seem to be shrinking back (implying: unto perdition)." I would hang my head and try not to let what they said stick, knowing they were ignorant of what they were speaking about. Still I would go forward for prayer at every opportunity. I would stand at the altar for long periods of time hoping against hope for a miracle.

I did all the right things spiritually: read my Bible, prayed, served in church, worshipped for hours, prayed with conviction, memorized scripture. I did all the right things physically: ate a perfect organic diet, no white flour, no soda, no sweets, no…… I took all the best supplements, drank only the purest water, etc. But still all my symptoms grew worse, my weight kept increasing, my hair fell out, my pain increased, my sleep got worse; I was constantly exhausted, overwhelmed, anxious and severely depressed.

At year seventeen, I gave up. I was tired of feeling guilty about not reading my Bible and praying every day and not doing all the things a good Christian wife and mom should do. My prayer life was reduced to whispering "please help me Jesus" or "please let me die God." The guilt was exhausting, and I could no longer shoulder it.

So I told God, "either you're God all by yourself and you do what you say you'll do, or not. Nothing I say or do can change that." I shared a hypothesis with God, "I actually believe in my heart of hearts that you ARE God and that you were telling the truth when you said you'd never leave me or forsake me, that you wouldn't allow me to be tempted beyond what I can withstand, that you'll take what the enemy means for my destruction and turn it for my good. I believe those things God and I'm going to stop DOING anything. I'm going to let go of all the "shoulds" and just exist the best I know how and see what happens. I can't get much worse than how I've been living and death would be a relief. So here it goes, God. I'm letting go. I'm giving up."

In December of the last year of my captivity, in the depth of suffocating depression, I finally made a conscious decision that suicide was no longer a choice even though I wanted more than anything to be in heaven. Years before, I had decided that everyone would be better off without me. But now I realized that while my husband could find a new wife, my girls could never find a new mom (the logic of a sick brain). I needed to be here for them no matter how damaged I was. I confessed to my husband some plans for taking my life that I had made in previous months, and the Lord gave me a life-changing revelation that my girls were graced by Him to have me as their mom. That revelation obliterated the guilt that had nearly consumed me about the damage I was causing in my girls' hearts and minds.

I talked with my husband, and we agreed it was time to acknowledge that we had seen only deteriorating physical and mental health for years, and we needed to face the possibility that I may never get better. My husband agreed to change his work schedule so he would be home earlier every day and help with the domestic duties, and we trudged on. I realized why God had me start homeschooling my girls several years before --it kept me alive. So, we settled in for the duration, choosing to believe that God is faithful. His promises are true and either we win here on earth or we win in glory, but either way we win.

Suddenly....

In January I saw a new doctor. The staff at the Seattle Pituitary Center began to tell us they thought I had a Human Growth Hormone (HGH) deficiency. I began to cry, and my husband's mouth fell open, as they listed about 25 symptoms. Chris said, "You just described my wife of the past 20 years." I had every single one of the symptoms they listed off! What a shock and relief to hear that someone might actually understand me. Tests were ordered that would confirm suspicions and if positive, the treatment was rather miraculous and would bring immediate improvements of nearly ALL symptoms!

The test was positive. I definitely had an HGH deficiency caused by a pituitary injury. WOW! Exactly twenty years, almost to the day from my initial brain injury, we had a possible cause for all my suffering. Could I begin to hope?

I began the daily injections and saw noticeable improvements on day two. It took us a little over a year and some pretty rough days to get the dosage right, but it has been worth the struggle. My depression left instantly, and only returned temporarily when we needed to make dosage adjustments. My anxiety has been nearly obliterated, and almost all other physical issues have vanished. It is miraculous, as the doctor said. God had not left me…. ever.

I look back now over all the pain and loss, the little memory of the early years of my second daughter, the fact that my husband truly deserves sainthood for enduring abuse and neglect, (the doctor actually commented how rare it is for a marriage to survive this condition. She said the fact that our marriage survived a 20 year HGH deficiency is truly extraordinary), and I have to say that the best part of the whole ordeal was also the worst. Those last three years when my physical and mental health were unbearably bad, was *when I finally gave up all my works of righteousness and even the guilt over not being able to do those works,* and chose to do nothing but exist, which really meant resting in God's promises.

In truth, when I consciously eliminated suicide as a choice, I had no other choice but to rest and trust that God was working on my behalf. It was then that I began to realize in my darkest hours, my darkest days and months, that **Jesus is who He says He is—Christ in me, the hope of glory**. He does in fact do ALL the things he says he will do. He brought relief. He brought answers. He brought restoration. He is redeeming the years that were eaten, stolen by darkness.

One of my biggest take-aways from my ordeal has been my total freedom from the works mentality that I existed in before. I used to pray so fervently for hours, I used to worship for hours, but I realize now that much of it was all about MY works. I so desperately wanted to be touched by God. I so desperately wanted to be healed. I thought if I prayed hard, loud and long, if I worshiped for hours on end, I could work up, deserve, or somehow coerce, God into touching me, delivering me, healing me. What I learned has changed me and changed my perspective of God. God has revealed to me that He is so good and His grace is easy. I just need to rest in Him.

Rest is the posture he intended for me because He's already completed the work. Grace isn't worked up or earned in any way. Grace is truly knowing every day that I am loved beyond what I could ever possibly earn. It's knowing that a simple heart-felt "thank you" or "help me" touches the heart of my Jesus more than hours of reading, singing and praying because "I should."

It's knowing that the God of the universe counted my hairs today because He loves me. It's knowing that He is working and praying on my behalf every minute of every day because He is so good. His goodness overwhelms me, and I've been swimming in grace for years, I just didn't always realize it. It's like when you carry your sleeping children to bed and tuck them in, and in the morning they wake up, and wonder how they got there.

Statistics tell us there are about 121 million people in the world suffering from depression and 1 million people commit suicide each year. It is my mission, to make it ok for fellow humans to share their darkness with me. We can choose not to feel threatened or run away scared when others share their addiction, abuse, depression or suicidal thoughts. You may have experienced unspeakable acts of violation as a child, or addictive behavior that seems to control you. Some have experienced deep betrayal or abandonment. We don't have all the answers, but we can listen, offer a hug, and pray to understand. We can introduce others to the One who does have the answers directly. The Bible tells us to weep with those who weep and to rejoice with those who rejoice. Let's determine to be good at both of these, even if we can't relate. At the end of the day, Jesus is there and He never leaves us.

Thank you, Bernece Teem, for sharing your story with us.

**Day Five**
**The Grand Finale!**

What a journey this has been! I hope that you have gleaned much from your personal trip through the book of Colossians.

I also hope that you know now, without a shadow of a doubt, "**Happy are the people whose God is the Lord!**" (Psalm 144:15)

This type of happiness is possible when Jesus is the center—or when He is *preeminent*—when He reigns supreme in all areas of our lives.

When I was in the midst of writing this study, a dear friend asked me if I could boil Colossians down to one thing, what would it be? I told her, the *preeminence of Jesus.*

This is the note we will end our *Live Happy* study on this week. As a final homework exercise, fill in the spaces below after looking up each verse. Write the phrase from the verse that reveals the preeminence of Jesus in each area.

### The Preeminence of Jesus –Colossians 1:18

**In Government:**

- Colossians 1:15:
- Colossians 1:16:
- Colossians 1:17:
- Colossians 1:18:


**In Restoring Relationships:**

- Colossians 1:21,22:
- Colossians 1:27:

**In Wisdom and Knowledge:**

- Colossians 2:2,3:
- Colossians 2:8:

**In Worship:**

- Colossians 2:11-13:
- Colossians 2:16-23:

**In Living Happy:**

- Colossians 3:1,3, 4:
- Colossians 3:5:

## *Praise God from Whom all blessings flow!*

Finish your study time today in worship and praise because Jesus is *in us,* and He enables us to *live happy*, as He is preeminent!

## About the Author:

Marjie Schaefer believes the Word of God is relevant, powerful, transformational, and life-giving to every single human being on the planet. She has spent her life investing in others and inviting them to join her in this pursuit of deeper truth.

As a result of her passion and pursuit, she has spent decades teaching women of all ages how to dig into the Word of God, and how to mine the treasures of it for themselves. She started in college and has continued on as a wife and mother, opening her heart and her home to those who hunger and thirst for more of God and His Word in their lives.

Marjie and her team currently lead the ministry**, Flourish Through the Word**, which is a community of women in the greater Seattle region committed to being equipped through God's Word. As a result of their time together in the Word, the women then move out into their arenas of influence, shining their lights for Jesus. You can find out more about this ministry, upcoming events and Bible studies, and the Flourish Conference at www.flourishthroughtheword.com. You can also sign up to receive regular email encouragements from Marjie.

Marjie has two previously published studies, _Grace Encounters_ and _Choose Joy._

Marjie has been married to Steve for 27 years and they have four children, a daughter Hayley, and sons Jordan, Matthew, and Luke.

## A Word of Thanks:

I am indebted to so many people for their help, support, encouragement and contributions to this Bible study.

My husband, Steve, enables and encourages me to study, write, teach and minister to others. I could not do what I do without his constant support. Thank you for impacting this study with your wisdom on fathering and life in the marketplace.

My fellow Flourish team-members, Vickie Adair and Lisa McKenney are invaluable to me. Vickie not only provided her story to be shared with others in this book, but she spent hours proof-reading the text and did all the bibliography research. Lisa is a gifted artist and creator-extraordinaire. Lisa is responsible for the beautiful graphics. Thank you, Vickie and Lisa for your contributions and your friendship.

Many thanks also to Bernece Teem and Marty Nystrom for their wonderful additions to *Live Happy*. Your input and wisdom has made this study all the more meaningful for each one of us.

Thanks also to Pam Sayre for her help in proof-reading the study.

And finally, thank you to my friends who came alongside and prayed for me and encouraged me as I studied and wrote *Live Happy*. You know who you are!

To God be all the glory!

# Works Cited

Achor, Shawn. *The Happiness Advantage: The Seven Principles of Positive Psychology That Fuel Success and Performance at Work*. New York: Crown Business, 2010. Print.

Hayford, Jack W. *New Spirit Filled Life Bible*. Nashville, TN: Thomas Nelson Bibles, 2002. Print.

Rosenberg, Joel C., and T. E. Koshy. *The Invested Life: Making Disciples of All Nations One Person at a Time*. Carol Stream, IL: Tyndale House, 2012. Print.

Rubin, Gretchen Craft. *The Happiness Project: Or Why I Spent a Year Trying to Sing in the Morning, Clean My Closets, Fight Right, Read Aristotle, and Generally Have More Fun*. New York: HarperCollins, 2009. Print.

Thompson, W. Oscar. *Concentric Circles of Concern*. Nashville, TN: Broadman, 1981. Print.

Tribole, Evelyn, and Elyse Resch. *Intuitive Eating*. New York: St. Martin's Griffin, 2012. Print.

Weiseth, Nish. *Speak: How Your Story Can Change the World*. Grand Rapids, MI: Zondervan, 2014. Print.

Wiersbe, Warren W., and Warren W. Wiersbe. *The Wiersbe Bible Commentary: The Complete New Testament in One Volume*. Colorado Springs, CO: David C. Cook, 2007. Print.

www.ingramcontent.com/pod-product-compliance
Lightning Source LLC
Chambersburg PA
CBHW070549300426
44113CB00011B/1835